Bullseye Brilliance: The Ultimate PDC Darts Quiz Book 2025

How to Use This Book

This book is designed for darts enthusiasts of all levels, whether you're a casual fan, an aspiring player, or a dedicated follower of the PDC. Here's how to get the most out of it:

1. **Quiz Yourself:** Each chapter contains trivia questions divided into three levels: Easy, Moderate, and Hard. Test your knowledge on your own or challenge a friend.

2. **Host a Quiz Night:** Use this book to host a darts-themed quiz night. Pick questions from different chapters to create a well-rounded challenge for your participants.

3. **Learn and Explore:** Use the answers at the end of each chapter to learn new facts and improve your darts knowledge. You can also dive into the history and strategies covered in the book.

4. **Customise Your Experience:** Start with your favourite chapter or follow the book from beginning to end. Each chapter covers a unique aspect of darts, ensuring there's something for everyone.

5. **Track Your Progress:** Revisit questions and see how much your knowledge improves over time. Use the "Hard" questions as benchmarks to measure your expertise.

Understanding Question Levels

Each chapter is structured with three levels of difficulty:

- **Easy:** These questions are perfect for beginners or casual fans. They cover foundational knowledge and widely known facts about darts.

- **Moderate:** For those with a deeper interest in darts, these questions challenge your understanding of the sport's players, tournaments, and history.

- **Hard:** Designed for darts experts, these questions delve into obscure details, records, and advanced knowledge that only dedicated fans are likely to know.

How to Use the Levels:

- Start with Easy questions to warm up or for a casual challenge. These are great for younger fans or those new to darts.

- Progress to Moderate questions as your confidence grows. These offer a balanced mix of fun and challenge.

- Test yourself with Hard questions to truly gauge your expertise or to compete with seasoned darts aficionados.

- Use the different levels to create diverse quiz rounds during a game night, ensuring fun for participants of all skill levels.

Whether you're preparing for a pub quiz, brushing up on darts history, or simply having fun, this book is your ultimate guide to all things darts. Enjoy!

Table of Contents

Chapter 1: The Legends of Darts

Chapter 2: The World Darts Championship

Chapter 3: Memorable Darts Moments

Chapter 4: Records and Statistics

Chapter 5: Iconic Rivalries

Chapter 6: Evolution of Darts Equipment

Chapter 7: The Premier League of Darts

Chapter 8: Top Darts Venues

Chapter 9: The Rise of International Darts

Chapter 10: Memorable Nine-Dart Finishes

Chapter 11: Famous Darts Personalities

Chapter 12: Darts Records and Achievements

Chapter 13: Darts Around the World

Chapter 14: Darts Innovations and Milestones

Chapter 15: Darts Legends Through the Years

Chapter 16: Memorable Matches and Moments

Chapter 17: Darts Strategies and Techniques

Chapter 18: Historical Darts Tournaments

Chapter 19: Luke Littler

Chapter 1: The Legends of Darts

Easy

1. Who is nicknamed "The Power" in darts?
2. What is the highest possible score with three darts?
3. Which country is Michael van Gerwen from?
4. What is the diameter of the dartboard's bullseye?
5. Who was the first darts player to win the PDC World Championship?
6. Which darts player is nicknamed "The Iceman"?
7. What is the total score needed to finish a leg in a standard game of darts?
8. Which player is known for his colourful mohawk hairstyles?
9. How many points is the green outer ring of the bullseye worth?
10. Who holds the record for the most PDC World Championship wins?

Moderate

11. Who was the first female player to compete in the PDC World Darts Championship?
12. What year did Raymond van Barneveld win his first PDC World Championship?
13. Name the tournament that features top players competing weekly across different venues.
14. Who is known as "The Flying Scotsman"?
15. What is the weight range for professional darts?
16. Which former champion has the nickname "Jackpot"?
17. How many points is a double ring worth if the dart lands in the double 20 section?
18. Which player was the first to win the World Matchplay three times in a row?
19. Who won the 2022 PDC World Darts Championship?
20. What is the official diameter of a darts board?

Hard

21. Who was the first player to hit a nine-dart finish on TV?
22. In which year was the Professional Darts Corporation (PDC) founded?
23. Who defeated Phil Taylor in the 2007 PDC World Championship final?
24. Name the first left-handed player to win the PDC World Darts Championship.
25. Who won the inaugural Grand Slam of Darts in 2007?
26. How many televised nine-dart finishes has Michael van Gerwen achieved as of 2024?
27. Which legendary player is nicknamed "Jaws"?
28. Which player hit a nine-dart finish in the 2021 PDC World Championship but still lost the match?
29. Who is the youngest player to win a PDC major title?

Chapter 1 Answers

Easy

1. Phil Taylor
2. 180
3. The Netherlands
4. 12.7 mm
5. Dennis Priestley
6. Gerwyn Price
7. 501
8. Peter Wright
9. 25 points
10. Phil Taylor (16 titles)

Moderate

11. Gayl King
12. 2007
13. Premier League Darts
14. Gary Anderson
15. 12 to 50 grams
16. Adrian Lewis
17. 40 points
18. Michael van Gerwen
19. Peter Wright
20. 451 mm

Hard

21. John Lowe
22. 1992
23. Raymond van Barneveld
24. Alan Warriner-Little
25. Phil Taylor
26. 24
27. Colin Lloyd
28. James Wade
29. Michael van Gerwen (aged 24)

Chapter 2: The World Darts Championship

Easy

1. Which event is considered the pinnacle of PDC darts?
2. Who won the first-ever PDC World Darts Championship?
3. In which month is the PDC World Darts Championship traditionally held?
4. What is the maximum number of sets played in a PDC World Darts Championship final?
5. Who won the PDC World Darts Championship in 2021?
6. What is the name of the trophy awarded to the PDC World Champion?
7. In what year did the PDC World Championship first take place?
8. What nationality is Gerwyn Price?
9. How many players compete in the first round of the PDC World Darts Championship?
10. What is the starting score for each player in a leg of darts?

Moderate

11. What venue hosts the PDC World Darts Championship?
12. Who was the first player to win the PDC World Darts Championship more than three times?
13. What is the format used to decide each match in the World Darts Championship?
14. Name the player who won the PDC World Darts Championship in 2014.
15. Who is the youngest ever PDC World Champion?
16. How much was the prize money for the 2023 PDC World Darts Champion?
17. Who holds the record for the most 180s scored in a single World Championship?
18. What year did the PDC World Darts Championship move to Alexandra Palace?
19. Which country has produced the most PDC World Champions?
20. Name the player who won the PDC World Darts Championship in 2020.

Hard

21. Name the first player to hit a nine-dart finish in the PDC World Championship.
22. What year did Fallon Sherrock make history by defeating two male players in the PDC World Championship?
23. Who holds the record for the highest average in a PDC World Championship match?
24. In what year did Phil Taylor last compete in the PDC World Championship?
25. Which player hit the first televised nine-dart finish at Alexandra Palace?
26. Name the player who defeated Michael van Gerwen in the 2022 PDC World Championship final.
27. Who is the first Japanese player to compete in the PDC World Championship?
28. Which legendary darts commentator was known for his iconic calls during World Championships?
29. What year did Rob Cross win the PDC World Championship?

Chapter 2 Answers

Easy

1. PDC World Darts Championship
2. Dennis Priestley
3. December/January
4. 13 sets
5. Gerwyn Price
6. Sid Waddell Trophy
7. 1994
8. Welsh
9. 96 players
10. 501

Moderate

11. Alexandra Palace
12. Phil Taylor
13. Sets format
14. Michael van Gerwen
15. Michael van Gerwen
16. £500,000
17. Gary Anderson
18. 2008
19. England
20. Peter Wright

Hard

21. Raymond van Barneveld
22. 2020
23. Michael van Gerwen
24. 2018
25. Adrian Lewis
26. Peter Wright
27. Haruki Muramatsu
28. Sid Waddell
29. 2018

Chapter 3: Memorable Darts Moments

Easy

1. Who hit a nine-dart finish during the 2021 World Matchplay?
2. What term is used for scoring three bullseyes in one turn?
3. Which darts player has the nickname "Mighty Mike"?
4. Who was the first player to win the World Grand Prix?
5. What is the highest score you can achieve with three darts?
6. Which legendary player is nicknamed "The Bronzed Adonis"?
7. What is the distance from the oche to the dartboard?
8. Who is the first female player to win a televised match in a PDC event?
9. What is the significance of the number 170 in darts?
10. Who won the Premier League Darts in 2020?

Moderate

11. Who scored the first televised nine-dart finish?
12. In which year was the first World Matchplay tournament held?
13. Name the player who won the inaugural Premier League Darts.
14. What year did Raymond van Barneveld defeat Phil Taylor in the World Championship final?
15. Who is known for his trademark celebration called "The Machine"?
16. How many darts are thrown in a perfect nine-dart finish?
17. Which event is traditionally held in Blackpool every summer?
18. Who is the only player to have won both the BDO and PDC World Championships in the same year?
19. How many points is the red bullseye worth?
20. Name the player who won the Grand Slam of Darts in 2019.

Hard

21. Name the first player to hit two nine-dart finishes in one match.
22. What year did the PDC World Cup of Darts debut?
23. Who holds the record for the most appearances in the PDC World Championship final?
24. Which player is nicknamed "Duzza"?
25. How many points does the outer ring of a treble score?
26. Who is the youngest player to appear in a PDC major final?
27. Name the player who hit a nine-dart finish in the 2021 PDC World Championship but still lost the match.
28. What is the smallest number of darts required to win a leg in 501 darts?
29. Who defeated Michael van Gerwen in the 2015 UK Open final?
30. Which iconic player retired after the 2018 PDC World Championship?

Chapter 3 Answers

Easy

1. Dimitri Van den Bergh
2. Hat Trick
3. Michael van Gerwen
4. Alan Warriner-Little
5. 180
6. Steve Beaton
7. 2.37 meters
8. Fallon Sherrock
9. The highest checkout
10. Glen Durrant

Moderate

11. John Lowe
12. 1994
13. Phil Taylor
14. 2007
15. James Wade
16. Nine
17. World Matchplay
18. Raymond van Barneveld
19. 50 points
20. Gerwyn Price

Hard

21. Phil Taylor
22. 2010
23. Phil Taylor
24. Glen Durrant
25. Triple the segment's number
26. Luke Littler
27. James Wade
28. Nine darts
29. Robert Thornton
30. Raymond van Barneveld

Chapter 4: Records and Statistics

Easy

1. What is the maximum checkout score in darts?
2. How many points is the outer bullseye worth?
3. How many segments does a standard dartboard have?
4. Which player has the record for most World Championship titles?
5. What is the minimum number of darts required to win a leg of 501?
6. Who was the first player to achieve a televised nine-dart finish?
7. What is the score needed to achieve a nine-dart finish in 501?

Moderate

8. Who holds the record for the highest average in a PDC match?
9. How many nine-dart finishes have been achieved in the PDC World Championship as of 2024?
10. What is the most common checkout combination in darts?
11. Which player has scored the most 180s in a single World Championship tournament?
12. What is the highest average ever recorded in a PDC World Championship final?
13. What is the smallest score that requires three darts to achieve?
14. Which player has won the Premier League Darts the most times?
15. What year was the first-ever televised nine-dart finish achieved?

Hard

16. Who holds the record for the most televised nine-dart finishes?
17. What is the record for the highest losing average in a PDC World Championship match?
18. Who was the first player to hit a nine-dart finish at Alexandra Palace?
19. Name the youngest player to achieve a televised nine-dart finish.
20. What is the record for the longest match in PDC World Championship history by legs played?
21. How many nine-dart finishes did Phil Taylor achieve during his career?
22. Who is the oldest player to win a PDC World Championship title?
23. What is the largest winning margin in a PDC World Championship final?
24. Who has the record for the fastest recorded leg of 501 darts?
25. How many darts are needed to achieve a perfect score of 501 using only the treble 20 segment?

Chapter 4 Answers

Easy

1. 170
2. 25 points
3. 20 segments
4. Phil Taylor
5. Nine darts
6. John Lowe
7. 501

Moderate

8. Michael van Gerwen
9. 12
10. Double 16
11. Gary Anderson
12. 114.05
13. 2
14. Phil Taylor
15. 1984

Hard

16. Phil Taylor
17. 108.86
18. Adrian Lewis
19. Michael van Gerwen
20. 50 legs
21. 11
22. John Part
23. 7 sets
24. Kyle Anderson
25. Nine darts

Chapter 5: Iconic Rivalries

Easy

1. Which two players are known for their iconic rivalry in the PDC World Championship finals during the 2000s?
2. Who is Phil Taylor's most famous rival?
3. Which player is nicknamed "Barney"?
4. What is the nationality of Michael van Gerwen?
5. Name the rivalry often called "The Battle of the Scots".
6. In which tournament did Fallon Sherrock defeat Mensur Suljović to create a historic upset?
7. Who was Raymond van Barneveld's first opponent in his PDC debut?
8. Which rivalry is known as "The Power vs. The Machine"?
9. Who defeated Adrian Lewis in the 2011 PDC World Championship final?
10. Name the rivalry where "Snakebite" and "Mighty Mike" frequently clashed.

Moderate

11. In which year did Gary Anderson defeat Michael van Gerwen to win his first PDC World Championship?
12. What is the name of the rivalry between Phil Taylor and Raymond van Barneveld?
13. Which two players were involved in a fiery exchange during the 2018 Grand Slam of Darts?
14. Who defeated Peter Wright in the 2022 Premier League Darts final?
15. What year did John Part defeat Phil Taylor in a World Championship final?
16. Name the rivalry between James Wade and Simon Whitlock that began in the World Matchplay.
17. Who defeated Michael Smith in the 2019 World Championship final?
18. Which two players faced off in the 2016 UK Open final?
19. Name the player who ended Phil Taylor's final World Championship run in 2018.
20. Who was Michael van Gerwen's opponent in his first World Championship victory?

Hard

21. In which year did Adrian Lewis and Gary Anderson face off in a World Championship final?
22. Name the rivalry often dubbed "The Dutch Duel".
23. Which player defeated Michael van Gerwen to win the 2017 UK Open?
24. Name the two players involved in the highest combined average match in PDC history.
25. Which two players are known for their tense rivalry during the Premier League Darts from 2015 to 2020?
26. Who defeated Rob Cross in the 2019 World Matchplay final?
27. What year did Peter Wright defeat Gerwyn Price in a televised final for the first time?
28. Name the rivalry between two players who faced off in multiple World Grand Prix finals during the 2010s.
29. In which year did James Wade defeat Adrian Lewis to win his only UK Open title?
30. Which two players are known for a rivalry spanning both the BDO and PDC eras?

Chapter 5 Answers

Easy

1. Phil Taylor and Raymond van Barneveld
2. Raymond van Barneveld
3. Raymond van Barneveld
4. Dutch
5. Gary Anderson vs. Peter Wright
6. PDC World Championship
7. Phil Taylor
8. Phil Taylor vs. James Wade
9. Gary Anderson
10. Peter Wright vs. Michael van Gerwen

Moderate

11. 2015
12. The Tungsten Titan Clash
13. Gerwyn Price and Gary Anderson
14. Jonny Clayton
15. 2003
16. "Wade vs. The Wizard"
17. Michael van Gerwen
18. Peter Wright and Michael van Gerwen
19. Rob Cross
20. Peter Wright

Hard

21. 2011
22. Michael van Gerwen vs. Raymond van Barneveld
23. Peter Wright
24. Michael van Gerwen and Gary Anderson
25. Michael van Gerwen and Gary Anderson
26. Rob Cross
27. 2019
28. Michael van Gerwen and Gary Anderson
29. 2008
30. Raymond van Barneveld and Phil Taylor

Chapter 6: Evolution of Darts Equipment

Easy

1. What material are modern professional dartboards typically made of?
2. What is the standard length of a dart from tip to tail?
3. What is the name of the section in the middle of the dartboard?
4. What is the most commonly used material for dart tips?
5. Which section of the dartboard is worth the most points?
6. What is the diameter of the inner bullseye?
7. What are dart stems typically made of?
8. What type of dart tip is used on electronic dartboards?
9. How many sections does a dartboard's double ring have?

Moderate

10. What was the traditional material used to make dartboards before sisal became popular?
11. What innovation did Unicorn introduce to dartboards in the 1990s?
12. What is the maximum allowed weight for a dart in PDC competitions?
13. What is the minimum diameter of a dartboard segment?
14. What type of dartboard is most commonly used in professional competitions?
15. Who introduced the first steel-tipped dart?
16. How are dartboard numbers traditionally arranged?
17. What is the standard thickness of a dart flight?

Hard

18. What innovation in darts design helped reduce bounce-outs in the 1980s?
19. What year was the first bristle dartboard introduced?
20. Who developed the modern tungsten alloy dart?
21. What is the purpose of "knurling" on dart barrels?
22. What is the recommended distance between the bullseye and the floor in professional darts?
23. What is the maximum diameter allowed for a dart barrel in PDC competitions?
24. What is the weight range for soft-tip darts?
25. What is the purpose of a "spinner" dart shaft?
26. How many grams does the heaviest legal PDC dart weigh?
27. What feature distinguishes "blade" dartboards from traditional wire dartboards?

Chapter 6 Answers

Easy

1. Sisal
2. 6 to 8 inches
3. The bullseye
4. Steel
5. Treble 20
6. 12.7 mm
7. Plastic or aluminium
8. Soft-tip
9. 20 sections

Moderate

10. Elm wood
11. Blade wiring
12. 50 grams
13. 8 mm
14. Bristle dartboard
15. Fred Dart
16. Randomised to reduce bias
17. 100 microns

Hard

18. Thin wiring with triangular edges
19. 1932
20. Conrad Daniels
21. To improve grip
22. 5 feet 8 inches (173 cm)
23. 7.9 mm
24. 14 to 20 grams
25. To allow flights to rotate on impact
26. 50 grams
27. Thin wiring to reduce bounce-outs

Chapter 7: The Premier League of Darts

Easy

1. In what year was the Premier League of Darts first held?
2. How many players typically compete in the Premier League of Darts?
3. What is the format used for Premier League matches?
4. Who won the inaugural Premier League of Darts title?
5. What day of the week are Premier League matches traditionally held?
6. Which player has won the most Premier League titles?
7. What is the maximum number of legs in a standard Premier League match?
8. Which venue hosted the Premier League final in 2023?
9. What is the prize for winning the Premier League of Darts?
10. Who was the first non-European player to compete in the Premier League?

Moderate

11. Which player has made the most consecutive Premier League appearances?
12. In which year did the Premier League introduce the "Judgement Night" format?
13. Who holds the record for the highest average in a Premier League match?
14. How many nights does the Premier League season typically last?
15. What year did Michael van Gerwen win his first Premier League title?
16. Which player was controversially left out of the 2021 Premier League lineup?
17. Name the first female player to compete in the Premier League of Darts.
18. Which player achieved a nine-dart finish during the 2020 Premier League?
19. How many points are awarded for a win in the Premier League?
20. Who won the Premier League in 2019?

Hard

21. Which two players contested the longest-ever Premier League match?
22. What is the record for the most 180s in a single Premier League season?
23. Who scored a nine-dart finish in the 2011 Premier League final?
24. Name the player with the most runner-up finishes in the Premier League.
25. In what year was the Premier League first broadcast on Sky Sports?
26. Which player scored the most points in the league stage but failed to win the title in 2020?
27. How many Premier League titles has Phil Taylor won?
28. What is the lowest average recorded in a Premier League match?
29. Who was the youngest player to win the Premier League title?
30. Name the player who defeated Raymond van Barneveld in his final Premier League match.

Chapter 7 Answers

Easy

1. 2005
2. 8-10 players
3. Best of 12 legs
4. Phil Taylor
5. Thursday
6. Phil Taylor
7. 12 legs
8. The O2 Arena, London
9. £250,000
10. Simon Whitlock

Moderate

11. Raymond van Barneveld
12. 2013
13. Michael van Gerwen (123.40)
14. 16 nights
15. 2013
16. Glen Durrant
17. Fallon Sherrock
18. Peter Wright
19. Two points
20. Michael van Gerwen

Hard

21. Gary Anderson and Michael van Gerwen
22. 79 (Michael van Gerwen)
23. Adrian Lewis
24. Raymond van Barneveld
25. 2005
26. Glen Durrant
27. Six
28. 72.75
29. Michael van Gerwen
30. Michael Smith

Chapter 8: Top Darts Venues

Easy

1. What is the name of the venue that hosts the PDC World Darts Championship?
2. In which city is the Winter Gardens, home of the World Matchplay, located?
3. What is the nickname of the Alexandra Palace venue?
4. Which country hosts the Premier League finals at the O2 Arena?
5. What is the name of the venue that hosts the UK Open?
6. Which arena hosted the inaugural PDC Premier League final?
7. In which German city is the European Championship held?
8. What iconic venue in Dublin hosts the World Grand Prix?
9. Where is the Dutch Darts Masters traditionally played?
10. What is the name of the venue that hosted the 2023 Grand Slam of Darts?

Moderate

11. What year did the PDC World Championship first move to Alexandra Palace?
12. Which venue is known as the "Mecca of Darts"?
13. What is the largest crowd ever recorded at a PDC event?
14. In which city is the Barnsley Metrodome, a popular venue for Pro Tour events, located?
15. Which venue hosted the first televised nine-dart finish?
16. Where is the Melbourne Darts Masters held?
17. Which venue in Las Vegas hosted the World Series of Darts?
18. What venue in Scotland is commonly used for PDC events?
19. What is the name of the venue that hosts the Champions League of Darts?

Hard

20. Which venue hosted the first-ever PDC World Darts Championship in 1994?
21. In what year did the Winter Gardens first host the World Matchplay?
22. Which venue was used for the inaugural European Darts Championship?
23. What is the name of the venue in Sydney that hosted the Sydney Darts Masters?
24. In which city is the PDC World Cup of Darts usually held?
25. Which venue in Germany regularly hosts the World Series of Darts Finals?
26. What is the seating capacity of the Alexandra Palace's main hall?
27. Which iconic venue hosted the 2007 World Darts Trophy?
28. Name the venue where the 2020 PDC Summer Series was held.
29. What is the name of the Irish venue that hosted the 2019 World Grand Prix?

Chapter 8 Answers

Easy

1. Alexandra Palace
2. Blackpool
3. Ally Pally
4. England
5. Butlin's Minehead
6. Wembley Arena
7. Dortmund
8. Citywest Hotel
9. Amsterdam
10. Aldersley Leisure Village

Moderate

11. 2008
12. Winter Gardens
13. 20,000
14. Barnsley
15. Jollees Cabaret Club
16. Margaret Court Arena
17. Mandalay Bay
18. The Hydro, Glasgow
19. Morningside Arena

Hard

20. Circus Tavern
21. 1994
22. Hilton Hotel, Frankfurt
23. Luna Park
24. Frankfurt
25. Salzburgarena
26. 10,400
27. De Bonte Wever, Assen
28. Marshall Arena, Milton Keynes
29. Citywest Hotel

Chapter 9: The Rise of International Darts

Easy

1. Which country is home to darts legend Michael van Gerwen?
2. Who was the first Australian player to compete in the PDC World Darts Championship?
3. What is the nickname of Canadian darts legend John Part?
4. Which Asian country hosts the Japan Darts Masters?
5. Who is the first player from Wales to win the PDC World Darts Championship?
6. In which country was the 2022 World Cup of Darts held?
7. What is the nationality of "The Flying Scotsman" Gary Anderson?
8. Name the first American player to reach the PDC World Championship.
9. Which African country has begun hosting darts tournaments since 2020?
10. Who is known as "The Dutch Destroyer"?

Moderate

11. What year did Fallon Sherrock become the first woman to win a match at the PDC World Championship?
12. Which Japanese player competed in the 2021 PDC World Darts Championship?
13. What is the highest finish ever recorded by a Chinese player in a PDC event?
14. Which Scandinavian country hosted the inaugural Nordic Darts Masters?
15. Name the Dutch player who won the PDC World Championship in 2007.
16. In what year did the World Series of Darts Finals debut in Australia?
17. What is the nationality of Deta Hedman, a trailblazer in women's darts?
18. Which player from New Zealand competed in the 2019 PDC World Championship?
19. What country is represented by players Damon Heta and Simon Whitlock?
20. Name the nation that Gerwyn Price represents in international darts.

Hard

21. What is the best finish achieved by an Indian player in a PDC World Championship?
22. Who was the first South African player to compete in a televised PDC event?
23. Name the first female player to win a match in the World Series of Darts.
24. Which nation hosted the inaugural World Cup of Darts in 2010?
25. What year did Singapore's Paul Lim hit a nine-dart finish in the BDO World Championship?
26. Name the only player from the Philippines to have competed in the PDC World Championship.
27. What is the best finish by a Canadian player in the PDC World Darts Championship?
28. Which Irish player reached the quarterfinals of the 2022 PDC World Darts Championship?
29. Who is the first German player to win a PDC Pro Tour event?
30. Name the venue in New Zealand that hosted the Auckland Darts Masters.

Chapter 9 Answers

Easy

1. The Netherlands
2. Simon Whitlock
3. Darth Maple
4. Japan
5. Gerwyn Price
6. Germany
7. Scotland
8. Danny Baggish
9. South Africa
10. Vincent van der Voort

Moderate

11. 2020
12. Seigo Asada
13. Last 32
14. Denmark
15. Raymond van Barneveld
16. 2013
17. Jamaican-British
18. Cody Harris
19. Australia
20. Wales

Hard

21. Last 64
22. Devon Petersen
23. Fallon Sherrock
24. England
25. 1990
26. Lourence Ilagan
27. Champion (John Part)
28. William O'Connor
29. Max Hopp
30. Trusts Arena

Chapter 10: Memorable Nine-Dart Finishes

Easy

1. What is a nine-dart finish in darts?
2. Who was the first player to hit a televised nine-dart finish?
3. In what year did Phil Taylor hit two nine-dart finishes in a single match?
4. How many darts are required to achieve a nine-dart finish?
5. Which player hit a nine-dart finish during the 2011 Premier League final?
6. What is the final score achieved when completing a nine-dart finish?
7. Who achieved the first nine-dart finish at the PDC World Championship?
8. What is the most common combination to complete a nine-dart finish?
9. Which player hit a nine-dart finish at the 2021 World Matchplay?
10. What term is often used to describe a perfect leg of darts?

Moderate

11. Who was the first female player to achieve a nine-dart finish in competition?
12. In what year did Michael van Gerwen hit a televised nine-dart finish for the first time?
13. Name the player who hit a nine-dart finish during the 2020 UK Open.
14. How many televised nine-dart finishes has Phil Taylor achieved?
15. Who hit a nine-dart finish in the 2022 PDC World Championship?
16. What is the prize typically awarded for a televised nine-dart finish?
17. Name the player who hit back-to-back nine-dart finishes in a Pro Tour event.
18. Who achieved the first nine-dart finish at the European Championship?
19. What is the highest recorded prize for a nine-dart finish in a PDC event?
20. Which country has seen the most televised nine-dart finishes?

Hard

21. Who holds the record for the fastest nine-dart finish in terms of dart speed?
22. Which player hit a nine-dart finish in the final of the 2008 World Matchplay?
23. Name the only player to achieve a nine-dart finish in the Grand Slam of Darts.
24. What year did Adrian Lewis hit his first nine-dart finish at the PDC World Championship?
25. Who hit a nine-dart finish in the 2019 Players Championship Finals?
26. Name the youngest player to hit a televised nine-dart finish.
27. How many nine-dart finishes were recorded during the 2017 PDC season?
28. Who hit a nine-dart finish at the 2020 World Grand Prix?
29. What is the longest recorded gap between two nine-dart finishes by the same player?
30. Name the player who hit a nine-dart finish during the 2006 Las Vegas Desert Classic.

Chapter 10 Answers

Easy

1. A Perfect leg of 501 darts completed in nine throws.
2. John Lowe
3. 2010
4. Nine
5. Adrian Lewis
6. 501
7. Raymond van Barneveld
8. 180, 180, and 141 (T20, T19, D12)
9. Dimitri Van den Bergh
10. Perfect leg

Moderate

11. Deta Hedman
12. 2012
13. Jonny Clayton
14. Eleven
15. James Wade
16. £50,000
17. Michael van Gerwen
18. Simon Whitlock
19. £100,000
20. England

Hard

21. Michael van Gerwen
22. Phil Taylor
23. Scott Waites
24. 2011
25. Chris Dobey
26. Luke Littler
27. Sixteen
28. Dirk van Duijvenbode
29. Ten years
30. Wes Newton

Chapter 11: Famous Darts Personalities

Easy

1. Who is nicknamed "The Power"?
2. Which player is known as "Mighty Mike"?
3. What is the nickname of Peter Wright?
4. Which darts legend is called "Barney"?
5. Who is referred to as "The Iceman"?
6. What is the nationality of Gerwyn Price?
7. Who is the Scottish player nicknamed "The Flying Scotsman"?
8. Which female darts player is nicknamed "The Queen of the Palace"?
9. Who is known as "Snakebite"?
10. What is the nickname of Adrian Lewis?

Moderate

11. What is the full name of "The Machine"?
12. Which player is nicknamed "The Wizard"?
13. Who is the first player to win 16 PDC World Championship titles?
14. Which Dutch player is nicknamed "The Cobra"?
15. Who is referred to as "The Rockstar"?
16. Which darts player is nicknamed "Duzza"?
17. What is the nationality of Devon Petersen, "The African Warrior"?
18. Who is known as "Hollywood"?
19. Which player is nicknamed "Voltage"?
20. What is the nickname of James Wade?

Hard

21. Who is "The Prince of Style"?
22. Name the Australian player nicknamed "The Original."
23. Who was called "Old Stoneface" in the early years of darts?
24. Which player is nicknamed "Yozza"?
25. Who is "The Gentle"?
26. What is the full name of the player known as "Rapid Ricky"?
27. Who is "The Titan"?
28. Which player is nicknamed "The Ferret"?
29. Who was "The Crafty Cockney"?
30. What is the nickname of Joe Cullen?

Chapter 11 Answers

Easy

1. Phil Taylor
2. Michael van Gerwen
3. Peter Wright
4. Raymond van Barneveld
5. Gerwyn Price
6. Welsh
7. Gary Anderson
8. Fallon Sherrock
9. Peter Wright
10. Jackpot

Moderate

11. James Wade
12. Simon Whitlock
13. Phil Taylor
14. Jelle Klaasen
15. Joe Cullen
16. Glen Durrant
17. South African
18. Chris Dobey
19. Rob Cross
20. The Machine

Hard

21. Rod Harrington
22. Kyle Anderson
23. John Lowe
24. Jamie Hughes
25. Mensur Suljovic
26. Ricky Evans
27. Andy Fordham
28. Jonny Clayton
29. Eric Bristow
30. The Rockstar

Chapter 12: Darts Records and Achievements

Easy

1. Who holds the record for the most PDC World Championship titles?
2. How many players are required to compete in the World Cup of Darts?
3. What is the fastest recorded leg of 501 darts?
4. What is the highest recorded average in a televised darts match?
5. How many 180s can be scored in a perfect nine-dart finish?
6. Which player achieved the first televised nine-dart finish?
7. How many sets are required to win the final match in the PDC World Darts Championship?

Moderate

8. Who was the youngest player to win a PDC World Championship?
9. How many points is the bullseye worth?
10. Which player has scored the most 180s in a single World Championship?
11. What is the longest match in PDC history by number of legs played?
12. Who is the oldest player to win a PDC World Championship?
13. What is the total prize fund for the PDC World Darts Championship as of 2024?
14. Name the first player to achieve a televised back-to-back nine-dart finish.
15. Who won the Premier League Darts title in 2021?

Hard

17. What is the lowest score that cannot be achieved with a single dart?
18. How many televised nine-dart finishes have been achieved as of 2024?
19. Which player holds the record for the most appearances in the PDC World Championship final?
20. Name the player who hit the most 180s in a single Premier League season.
21. What is the longest recorded gap between two nine-dart finishes by a single player?
22. Who holds the record for the highest losing average in a PDC World Championship match?
23. What is the record for the most 180s scored in a single PDC World Championship tournament?
24. Who hit a nine-dart finish in the 2015 UK Open final?
25. Name the first player to win the Grand Slam of Darts.
26. What year did Michael van Gerwen achieve his first televised nine-dart finish?

Chapter 12 Answers

Easy

1. Phil Taylor
2. Two players per team
3. 9 darts
4. 123.40 (Michael van Gerwen)
5. Three
6. John Lowe
7. Seven sets

Moderate

8. Michael van Gerwen
9. 50 points
10. Gary Anderson
11. 50 legs
12. John Part
13. £2.5 million
14. Phil Taylor
15. Jonny Clayton

Hard

17. 23
18. 76
19. Phil Taylor
20. Michael van Gerwen
21. Ten years
22. Raymond van Barneveld (108.86)
23. 71
24. Michael van Gerwen
25. Phil Taylor
26. 2012

Chapter 13: Darts Around the World

Easy

1. Which country hosts the Japan Darts Masters?
2. Who is the first Canadian player to win a PDC World Darts Championship?
3. What is the nickname of the South African darts player Devon Petersen?
4. Name the first country to win the PDC World Cup of Darts.
5. In which city is the Melbourne Darts Masters held?
6. Which player from Singapore famously hit a nine-dart finish in the BDO World Championship?
7. What is the official governing body for professional darts in Germany?
8. Name the New Zealand player who participated in the 2021 World Darts Championship.
9. Which country is represented by Damon Heta in international darts?
10. Who is the first Japanese player to qualify for the PDC World Championship?

Moderate

11. In which Scandinavian country is the Nordic Darts Masters held?
12. What is the name of the venue in Australia that hosts the Sydney Darts Masters?
13. Which player was the first to represent India in the PDC World Darts Championship?
14. What year did Paul Lim compete in his first PDC World Championship?
15. Name the first Irish player to win a PDC event.
16. What is the nickname of the Dutch darts player Dirk van Duijvenbode?
17. Which American player reached the quarterfinals of the 2022 PDC World Darts Championship?
18. What is the name of the professional darts league in China?
19. Who was the first Australian player to win the World Series of Darts Finals?
20. Which venue in Germany hosts the European Championship of Darts?

Hard

21. Who is the only player from the Philippines to compete in the PDC World Championship?
22. What is the highest finish achieved by a South American player in a PDC event?
23. Which nation has produced the most female darts players in international competitions?
24. Name the first German player to reach the semifinals of a major PDC tournament.
25. What year did Singapore first compete in the PDC World Cup of Darts?
26. Which country hosts the Gibraltar Darts Trophy?
27. Name the player who became the first Asian champion in a PDC-affiliated event.
28. What is the nickname of the Canadian player Jeff Smith?
29. Which venue in Las Vegas hosted the inaugural World Series of Darts event?
30. Who was the first Welsh player to win the World Matchplay?

Chapter 13 Answers

Easy

1. Japan
2. John Part
3. The African Warrior
4. England
5. Melbourne
6. Paul Lim
7. Deutscher Dart-Verband (DDV)
8. Ben Robb
9. Australia
10. Haruki Muramatsu

Moderate

11. Denmark
12. Luna Park
13. Nitin Kumar
14. 2012
15. William O'Connor
16. The Titan
17. Danny Baggish
18. China Darts League (CDL)
19. Damon Heta
20. Westfalenhalle, Dortmund

Hard

21. Lourence Ilagan
22. Quarterfinals
23. England
24. Gabriel Clemens
25. 2014
26. Gibraltar
27. Seigo Asada
28. The Silencer
29. Mandalay Bay
30. Gerwyn Price

Chapter 14: Darts Innovations and Milestones

Easy

1. What material is commonly used to make modern dart barrels?
2. What is the standard distance from the oche to the dartboard in professional darts?
3. What is the purpose of flights on a dart?
4. When was the PDC (Professional Darts Corporation) established?
5. What is the official diameter of the dartboard bullseye?
6. Who introduced the first steel-tipped darts?
7. What is the standard weight range for professional darts?
8. Name the innovation introduced to dartboards to reduce bounce-outs.
9. What is the official height from the floor to the bullseye in darts?
10. What type of dartboard is used in most professional competitions?

Moderate

11. Which company is the official supplier of dartboards for the PDC?
12. What innovation did the Unicorn Eclipse dartboard introduce?
13. What is the purpose of knurling on a dart barrel?
14. Which PDC-affiliated event was the first to use electronic scoring systems?
15. What material is commonly used for premium dart shafts?
16. What feature differentiates "blade" dartboards from traditional wired dartboards?
17. Which type of darts is used for electronic dartboards?
18. When did the first televised darts match air?

Hard

19. Who developed the modern tungsten dart?
20. What is the smallest possible diameter of a dart barrel allowed in PDC competitions?
21. What year did Winmau introduce the "Blade 5" dartboard?
22. Which innovation in dart flights is designed to reduce air drag?
23. What is the maximum weight allowed for a dart in professional competition?
24. Name the first venue to use bristle dartboards for televised matches.
25. What is the highest recorded average in a PDC match using the Unicorn Eclipse dartboard?
26. What year did "spinner shafts" become a standard accessory in professional darts?
27. Who introduced "tapered barrels" in modern dart design?
28. What is the maximum allowed length for a dart used in PDC competition?

Chapter 14 Answers

Easy

1. Tungsten
2. 2.37 meters
3. To stabilise the dart in flight
4. 1992
5. 12.7 mm
6. Fred Dart
7. 18-50 grams
8. Blade wiring
9. 1.73 meters
10. Bristle dartboard

Moderate

11. Winmau
12. Thin blade wiring
13. To improve grip and control
14. World Series of Darts
15. Carbon fibre
16. Wiring embedded in the board
17. Soft-tip darts
18. 1937

Hard

19. Conrad Daniels
20. 6 mm
21. 2016
22. Winged flights
23. 50 grams
24. Jollees Cabaret Club
25. 123.5
26. 2005
27. Alan Glazier
28. 30.5 cm

Chapter 15: Darts Legends Through the Years

Easy

1. Who is nicknamed "The Crafty Cockney"?
2. Which player is famously known as "The Iceman"?
3. Name the Scottish player nicknamed "The Flying Scotsman."
4. Which darts legend has the nickname "The Bronzed Adonis"?
5. What is the nationality of the player known as "Snakebite"?
6. Who is nicknamed "The Silencer"?
7. What is the nickname of Simon Whitlock?
8. Which darts player is referred to as "Darth Maple"?
9. Name the first player to win both the BDO and PDC World Championships.
10. Who is the legendary darts commentator known for popularising the sport on TV?

Moderate

11. What is the nickname of the Dutch player Jelle Klaasen?
12. Which darts player is nicknamed "The Wizard"?
13. Who is known as "The Machine"?
14. What is the nickname of the player Glen Durrant?
15. Which darts player is nicknamed "Voltage"?
16. Who was nicknamed "Old Stoneface"?
17. Which player is referred to as "Hollywood"?
18. Name the player known as "The Rockstar."
19. Who was nicknamed "The Prince of Style"?

Hard

20. Which player was the first to win the Grand Slam of Darts?
21. What is the nickname of the Australian player Kyle Anderson?
22. Name the player known as "The Titan."
23. Which player is nicknamed "Rapid Ricky"?
24. Who was the first darts player to be knighted?
25. What is the nickname of Jamie Hughes?
26. Name the Austrian player referred to as "The Gentle."
27. Who was known as "The King of Bling"?
28. What nickname is associated with darts legend Alan Evans?
29. Name the player known as "The Lion King."

Chapter 15 Answers

Easy

1. Eric Bristow
2. Gerwyn Price
3. Gary Anderson
4. Steve Beaton
5. Scottish
6. Jeff Smith
7. The Wizard
8. John Part
9. Raymond van Barneveld
10. Sid Waddell

Moderate

11. The Cobra
12. Simon Whitlock
13. James Wade
14. Duzza
15. Rob Cross
16. John Lowe
17. Chris Dobey
18. Joe Cullen
19. Rod Harrington

Hard

20. Phil Taylor
21. The Original
22. Andy Fordham
23. Ricky Evans
24. Sir John Lowe
25. Yozza
26. Mensur Suljović
27. Bobby George
28. Evz
29. Mark Webster

Chapter 16: Memorable Matches and Moments

Easy

1. Who won the 2020 PDC World Championship?
2. Which player defeated Phil Taylor in his final PDC World Championship match?
3. Name the venue where the PDC World Darts Championship is held.
4. Which player hit a nine-dart finish during the 2022 Premier League Darts?
5. Who defeated Michael van Gerwen in the 2019 World Matchplay final?
6. Which darts player famously won the 2018 World Championship as a debutant?
7. Who is the reigning champion of the 2023 Grand Slam of Darts?
8. Which country won the 2021 World Cup of Darts?

Moderate

9. What was the first year the PDC World Darts Championship was held at Alexandra Palace?
10. Name the player who defeated Peter Wright in the 2021 Premier League Darts final.
11. Who scored the most 180s in a single PDC World Darts Championship tournament?
12. Which player holds the record for the highest televised average in darts?
13. Name the first player to achieve back-to-back nine-dart finishes in a televised match.
14. In what year did Rob Cross defeat Phil Taylor to win the PDC World Darts Championship?
15. Who won the inaugural World Series of Darts Finals?
16. Which player famously hit a nine-dart finish during the 2009 UK Open but lost the match?
17. Who won the 2020 World Matchplay in Milton Keynes?
18. Name the player who defeated Gary Anderson in the 2021 PDC World Championship final.

Hard

19. Which player defeated Raymond van Barneveld in his farewell PDC World Championship match?
20. Name the first player to hit a nine-dart finish in the Grand Slam of Darts.
21. What is the longest match by legs played in PDC World Championship history?
22. Who was the first player to defeat Phil Taylor in a World Matchplay final?
23. Name the player who scored a nine-dart finish during the 2007 Las Vegas Desert Classic.
24. Which player achieved the highest losing average in a PDC World Championship match?
25. In what year did Adrian Lewis achieve his first nine-dart finish in the PDC World Championship?
26. Name the only player to hit two nine-dart finishes in a single Premier League season.
27. Who won the 2016 Champions League of Darts?
28. Which player holds the record for the most 180s in a single PDC World Championship final?

Chapter 16 Answers

Easy

1. Peter Wright
2. Rob Cross
3. Alexandra Palace
4. Jonny Clayton
5. Rob Cross
6. Rob Cross
7. Michael Smith
8. Scotland

Moderate

9. 2008
10. Jonny Clayton
11. Gary Anderson
12. Michael van Gerwen (123.40)
13. Phil Taylor
14. 2018
15. Michael van Gerwen
16. Mervyn King
17. Dimitri Van den Bergh
18. Gerwyn Price

Hard

19. Darin Young
20. Scott Waites
21. 50 legs
22. Larry Butler
23. Raymond van Barneveld
24. Raymond van Barneveld (108.86)
25. 2011
26. Michael van Gerwen
27. Phil Taylor
28. Michael Smith

Chapter 17: Darts Strategies and Techniques

Easy

1. What is the main goal of scoring in 501 darts?
2. Which section of the dartboard is worth triple the segment's value?
3. What is the recommended stance for throwing darts?
4. Name the grip technique where all three fingers hold the barrel.
5. What is the most commonly targeted segment for high scores?
6. What is the term for finishing a game with a double?
7. Which throw is considered the "perfect setup" for a nine-dart finish?
8. What is the term for missing the outer bullseye and hitting the inner ring?
9. What is the best strategy to hit a double 20 consistently?
10. How many darts are thrown in a single turn in standard play?

Moderate

11. What is the name of the technique used to align the shoulder and arm with the dartboard?
12. Which segment is commonly used to reduce the score to an even number?
13. What is the term for a score of three darts totalling 26 points?
14. What is the optimal weight range for darts to improve accuracy?
15. Name the technique where a player aims for the bullseye for a more central throw.
16. What is the significance of leaving a "double out" in professional darts?
17. Which type of dart shaft is known for providing a lighter throw?
18. What strategy is often employed to avoid leaving a score of one?
19. What is the recommended height for a dartboard in soft-tip darts?
20. Which finishing double is considered easiest for right-handed players?

Hard

21. Name the advanced grip style where the thumb rests against the side of the barrel.
22. What is the ideal trajectory angle for a dart to minimise bounce-outs?
23. Which segment is targeted to reduce a score of 57 to an even double-out finish?
24. What is the recommended follow-through action after releasing a dart?
25. Name the psychological technique players use to maintain focus during high-pressure moments.
26. What is the term for scoring three darts in the same treble segment?
27. Which flight shape is considered best for stability in a slow throw?
28. Name the technique where a player intentionally hits a single to set up a preferred double.
29. Which hand position is recommended for a player using heavier darts?
30. What is the optimal distance between the dart tip and the board upon release?

Chapter 17 Answers

Easy

1. Reduce the score to zero.
2. Treble ring.
3. Sideways with dominant foot forward.
4. Three-finger grip.
5. Treble 20.
6. Checkout.
7. Two 180s.
8. Outer bull.
9. Steady aim and consistent release.
10. Three darts.

Moderate

11. Shoulder alignment.
12. Treble 17.
13. "Bed and breakfast."
14. 18-24 grams.
15. Bullseye alignment.
16. It ensures a winning throw.
17. Plastic or nylon shafts.
18. Aim for a segment divisible by two.
19. 5 feet 8 inches.
20. Double 16.

Hard

21. Pencil grip.
22. 30-45 degrees.
23. Treble 19.
24. Extend the arm fully toward the board.
25. Visualisation.
26. Maximum or "180."
27. Kite-shaped flights.
28. Setup shot.
29. Relaxed yet firm grip.
30. 2-3 millimetres.

Chapter 18: Historical Darts Tournaments

Easy

1. What year was the first PDC World Darts Championship held?
2. Which tournament is known as the "FA Cup of Darts"?
3. What is the name of the venue where the World Matchplay is traditionally held?
4. Which darts tournament is played at the Alexandra Palace every December?
5. Who was the inaugural winner of the Grand Slam of Darts?
6. Which event pits two-player teams against each other in a country-versus-country format?
7. Name the tournament known for its double-start format.
8. In which month is the Premier League Darts final traditionally held?
9. What is the name of the tournament that features top players competing across weekly venues?
10. Which darts tournament was first held in Blackpool in 1994?

Moderate

11. What year was the UK Open first played?
12. Which tournament debuted in Germany in 2008 as a major PDC event?
13. Who won the first-ever European Championship of Darts?
14. Which venue hosted the inaugural Champions League of Darts?
15. Name the first country to host the World Series of Darts Finals.
16. Which player won the 2019 World Cup of Darts for Scotland alongside Gary Anderson?
17. What year was the first PDC World Cup of Darts held?
18. Which country hosts the Nordic Darts Masters?
19. Name the tournament played annually in Wolverhampton.
20. What year was the Grand Slam of Darts introduced?

Hard

21. Which player won the inaugural World Matchplay in 1994?
22. What year did the Las Vegas Desert Classic debut?
23. Name the first female player to compete in the Grand Slam of Darts.
24. Which player won the 2022 European Championship of Darts?
25. What year did the Champions League of Darts debut?
26. Which player achieved the most 180s in a single Grand Slam of Darts tournament?
27. Name the first player to win the UK Open three times.
28. What year was the Players Championship Finals introduced?
29. Which venue hosted the final of the 2021 World Series of Darts Finals?
30. Who won the inaugural PDC World Darts Championship in 1994?

Chapter 18 Answers

Easy

1. 1994
2. UK Open
3. Winter Gardens
4. PDC World Darts Championship
5. Phil Taylor
6. World Cup of Darts
7. World Grand Prix
8. May
9. Premier League Darts
10. World Matchplay

Moderate

11. 2003
12. European Championship
13. Phil Taylor
14. Motorpoint Arena, Cardiff
15. Scotland
16. Peter Wright
17. 2010
18. Denmark
19. Grand Slam of Darts
20. 2007

Hard

21. Larry Butler
22. 2002
23. Anastasia Dobromyslova
24. Ross Smith
25. 2016
26. Michael van Gerwen
27. Phil Taylor
28. 2009
29. AFAS Live, Amsterdam
30. Dennis Priestley

Chapter 19: Luke Littler

Easy Section

1. What year was Luke Littler born?
2. What nickname is Luke Littler known by in darts?
3. Which country does Luke Littler represent in darts?
4. At what age did Luke Littler win his first major darts title?
5. What is Luke Littler's throwing hand – left or right?
6. In which competition did Luke Littler make his debut in the PDC?
7. What brand of darts does Luke Littler use?
8. Which youth championship did Luke Littler famously win?
9. What colour is commonly associated with Luke Littler's darts flights?
10. Luke Littler plays in which darts organization?

Moderate Section

11. What was the first televised tournament in which Luke Littler participated?
12. In which year did Luke Littler first qualify for a PDC event?
13. What is Luke Littler's highest three-dart average in a competitive match?
14. Which dart legend has publicly praised Luke Littler's potential?
15. Luke Littler is considered a prodigy. At what age did he first hit a 9-darter in competition?
16. What is Luke Littler's best performance in the WDF World Championship?
17. How many major youth titles has Luke Littler won as of 2024?
18. Luke Littler's nickname refers to which mythical creature?
19. In which year did Luke Littler start competing in senior-level events?
20. What is Luke Littler's walk-on song?

Hard Section

21. What exact weight are Luke Littler's darts?
22. In what round did Luke Littler exit during his debut senior-level televised event?
23. Who was Luke Littler's opponent in his first televised senior-level match?
24. What was Luke Littler's winning average in the final of his first major youth title?
25. Luke Littler broke a record for being the youngest player to achieve what milestone in professional darts?
26. Against which opponent did Luke Littler record his first 100+ average in senior competition?
27. What is the highest recorded checkout Luke Littler has achieved in a professional match?
28. In which European country did Luke Littler win his first international title?
29. How many maximums (180s) did Luke Littler hit in his debut PDC event?
30. Who was Luke Littler's doubles partner in his first pairs competition victory?

Answers Chapter 19

Easy Section

1. 2007
2. The Nuke
3. England
4. 14
5. Right
6. UK Open
7. Red Dragon
8. JDC World Championship
9. Black and orange
10. PDC (Professional Darts Corporation)

Moderate Section

11. WDF World Championship
12. 2023
13. 112.5
14. Phil Taylor
15. 13 years old
16. Semi-finalist
17. 3
18. A nuclear bomb (The Nuke)
19. 2023
20. Greenlight by Pitbull Ft Florida

Hard Section

21. 23 grams
22. Third round
23. Joe Cullen
24. 102.7
25. Youngest player to hit a 9-darter in a senior competition
26. Nathan Aspinall
27. 161
28. Netherlands
29. 12
30. Alfie Thompson